Voices for Green Choices

Rachel Carson

Fighting Pesticides and Other Chemical Pollutants

By Patricia Lantier

Crabtree Publishing Company

www.crabtreebooks.com

Crabtree Publishing Company

Author: Patricia Lantier
Publishing plan research and development:
 Sean Charlebois, Reagan Miller
 Crabtree Publishing Company
Editor: Lynn Peppas
Proofreader: Crystal Sikkens
Project coordinator: Robert Walker
Content and curriculum adviser: Suzy Gazlay, M.A.
Editorial: Mark Sachner
Photo research: Ruth Owen
Design: Westgraphix/Tammy West
Production coordinator: Margaret Amy Salter
Prepress technicians: Margaret Amy Salter, Ken Wright
Written, developed, and produced by Water Buffalo Books

Cover photo: As a scientist, Rachel Carson was devoted
to saving life on our planet. As a writer, she infused
even her most dire warnings about the condition of
the environment with a poetic sensibility that drew its beauty
from her love for aquatic life.

Photo credits:
Alamy: Lee Karen Stow: page 15 (bottom)
AP Photos: page 7 (bottom); page 30 (bottom); page
 40 (bottom)
Corbis: Bettmann: pages 9 (bottom), 24 (top), 36 (bottom),
39 (top); JP Laffont/Sygma: page 38 (bottom)
FLPA: Wayne Hutchinson: front cover (main); S & D & K
 Maslowski: page 4 (left); Frans Lanting: page
 6 (bottom); Bernd Zoller: page 9 (bottom); Wil
 Meinderts: page 27 (right bottom)
Getty Images: CBS Photo Archive: page 5 (bottom);
 Alfred Eisenstaedt: pages 13 (bottom), 21 (top),
 24 (bottom), 35 (right), 41 (right); Hank Walker:
 page 21 (bottom)
The Lear/Carson Collection, Connecticut College:
 front cover (inset), pages 1, 9 (top), 10 (left),
 12 (bottom right), 17 (bottom), 20 (top), 23 (top),
 31 (right)
Library of Congress: image 3g05869u: page 14 (left)
Magnum Photos: Erich Hartmann: pages 26 (left),
 33 (top)
Public domain: page 16 (bottom)
Rachel Carson Archives, Chatham University, Pittsburgh,
 PA: pages 19 (bottom), 20 (bottom)
Rachel Carson National Wildlife Refuge: page 29 (top)
Shutterstock: pages 11 (bottom), 12 (left), 18 (left),
 22 (bottom), 25 (left), 27 (top and center), 34 (left),
 37 (bottom), 41 (bottom), 42 (bottom)
U.S. Fish & Wildlife Service: pages 28, 32 (bottom)
Wikimedia Commons: Rachel Carson Homestead,
 Springdale, PA: page 11 (right)

Library and Archives Canada Cataloguing in Publication

Lantier, Patricia, 1952-
 Rachel Carson : fighting pesticides and other chemical
pollutants / Patricia Lantier.

(Voices for green choices)
Includes index.
ISBN 978-0-7787-4663-8 (bound).--ISBN 978-0-7787-4676-8 (pbk.)

 1. Carson, Rachel, 1907-1964--Juvenile literature.
2. Biologists--United States--Biography--Juvenile literature.
3. Environmentalists--United States--Biography—Juvenile
literature. I. Title. II. Series: Voices for green choices

QH31.C33L35 2009   j333.95'16092   C2009-900029-6

Library of Congress Cataloging-in-Publication Data

Lantier, Patricia, 1952-
 Rachel Carson : fighting pesticides and other chemical pollutants
/ by Patricia Lantier.
   p. cm. -- (Voices for green choices)
 Includes index.
 ISBN 978-0-7787-4676-8 (pbk. : alk. paper)
-- ISBN 978-0-7787-4663-8 (reinforced library binding : alk. paper)
 1. Carson, Rachel, 1907-1964--Juvenile literature. 2. Biologists--
United States--Biography--Juvenile literature. 3. Environmental-
ists--United States--Biography--Juvenile literature. I. Title.

QH31.C33L37 2009
333.95'16092--dc22
[B]
                                              2008054511

Crabtree Publishing Company

www.crabtreebooks.com   1-800-387-7650

Printed in Canada/112018/MQ20181026

Published in Canada
Crabtree Publishing
616 Welland Ave.
St. Catharines, Ontario
L2M 5V6

Published in the United States
Crabtree Publishing
PMB 59051
350 Fifth Avenue, 59th Floor
New York, New York 10118

Published in the United Kingdom
Crabtree Publishing
Maritime House
Basin Road North, Hove
BN41 1WR

Published in Australia
Crabtree Publishing
3 Charles Street
Coburg North
VIC, 3058

Contents

Chapter 1

A Clear Voice for Life on Earth

Thousands of Americans gathered in front of their televisions on the evening of April 3, 1963. They waited with great interest to watch a CBS News special program titled, "The Silent Spring of Rachel Carson." The program focused on a controversial book about the dangers of pesticides. The author, Rachel Carson, was a well-known marine biologist and writer. She was a featured guest on the program. *Silent Spring* was Rachel's fourth book. Published a year earlier, it had drawn a quick and strong response from the American people.

A Shocking Message

More than 250,000 copies of *Silent Spring* had sold in the first four months after its release. Six hundred thousand copies sold in the first year. People across the country were concerned about Miss Carson's message. During the CBS program, she read from her book. She defended the accuracy of her information. She explained how big companies and the United States Department of Agriculture used pesticides and other chemicals to exterminate insect pests. The companies were using one particular pesticide—DDT—in an especially reckless manner. They sprayed this poison and other chemicals without thinking or caring about

▲ In her book *Silent Spring*, Rachel Carson encouraged readers to explore and enjoy the beauty of nature. She also cautioned them to protect Earth's fragile life forms and environment from the use of chemicals that would eventually destroy our world. Animals, plants, even humans, might no longer exist, and the melodious sounds of spring would be gone forever.

the terrible damage they were also inflicting on other forms of life and the environment.

Rachel was ill during the taping of the program. In fact, she had been ill during the four long years it took her to write *Silent Spring*, but she had courage and a mission to accomplish. Television allowed her to share her message with millions of people. Americans needed to know the truth. Insects were not the only forms of life at risk from pesticide use. All life, including human life, was in danger. The pesticides killed plants and animals. They polluted the soil, the air, and the waterways. They made people sick. If people continued to use these poisons, they might one day wake up to a permanently silent spring, one without the sounds of birds singing or leaves rustling in the trees, and without people to hear them. The use of pesticides and other chemicals had to be controlled. Americans were shocked by this information.

"We still talk in terms of conquest. We still haven't become mature enough to think of ourselves as only a tiny part of a vast and incredible universe. Man's attitude toward nature is today critically important simply because we have now acquired a fateful power to alter and destroy nature. But man is a part of nature and his war against nature is inevitably a war against himself."

- Rachel Carson, speaking at the end of her television interview in 1963

◄ News reporter Eric Sevareid talks to Rachel Carson about her controversial book *Silent Spring*. The interview was part of a *CBS Reports* program titled "The Silent Spring of Rachel Carson." The special event, which aired April 3, 1963, gave Rachel an opportunity to bring her message to millions of people.

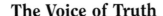

Respect for All

For as long as she could remember, Rachel had loved and respected all the elements of nature. She believed Earth's plants and animals each have a purpose. In her view, the planet is a huge community of living organisms that depend on each other to survive. Humans are a part of this community of life. With this in mind, humans must realize the value of all living things. They should do their best to protect all forms of life as well as Earth's environment and resources.

The Voice of Truth

Pesticides were being sprayed without people's permission. Chemical manufacturers had assured everyone that the pesticides were safe. Now the public wanted to know more, and demanded answers to their questions.

Immediately following the publication of *Silent Spring*, industry leaders claimed that Rachel's research and information were inaccurate. They said she was causing trouble over nothing.

The country was in an uproar. CBS News decided to invite Rachel to tell her story on television. Americans could finally "meet" the person who had written such beautiful books about the sea, and who now warned that pesticides were poisoning them. CBS also invited industry leaders and government agency representatives to explain their positions. In a series of taped interviews, both sides of the pesticide issue had a chance to state their cases.

Rachel Carson calmly presented her views and evidence. She was soft-spoken, but determined to make her point. The strength of a life's career as a scientist, writer, and naturalist supported her claims.

◀ Pesticides affected bird life in many ways. This photo shows two healthy peregrine falcon eggs alongside other eggs terribly affected by DDT poisoning.

A Concerned Professional

At first, Rachel's opponents on the TV special said the information in her book was wrong. They called her an alarmist. They even questioned her ability as a scientist because she was a woman. But Rachel's information was not wrong. It was accurate, and the businessmen and government officials had to admit they had been careless. They also agreed that pesticides and other chemicals should be used more carefully.

In "The Silent Spring of Rachel Carson," Rachel showed clearly that she was a concerned professional. Her claims were based on facts. She had consulted with hundreds of other scientists and experts for her book. It had taken several years to gather accurate information and testimony. The public needed to be aware of the dangers of pesticide use. Rachel Carson's warning was taken seriously. The years of careful research had been worth the time.

Rachel also believed that humans should not try to control the rest of the natural world. Her previous books reflected her lifelong passion for the

▶ Rachel Carson holds a copy of *Silent Spring* in her study in Silver Spring, Maryland, in 1963. She wrote this book to alert the American public to the dangers of pesticides and other chemical pollutants.

Nothing but the Truth

Rachel Carson won the National Book Award for Nonfiction for *Silent Spring*. She felt privileged to receive this honor. In her acceptance speech, Rachel stated, "The aim of science is to discover and illuminate truth. And that, I take it, is the aim of literature, whether biography or history or fiction. It seems to me, then, that there can be no separate literature of science."

Rachel was a scientist who also loved to write. Science provided her with a wonderful subject for her writing. Her remarkable books showed people that science as literature worked beautifully to present the truth about life.

infinite mysteries of the sea. Her writing introduced readers to the astounding beauty of the natural world, in an eloquent and poetic voice.

Sounding an Alarm

The time had come to awaken people to a harsh reality. Nature was in danger. Its bounty should be treated with respect and protected for future generations. Humans had to change their attitudes. They must learn to live in harmony with their environment and all living things.

Silent Spring had a profound impact on the United States and the rest of the world. In the early 1960s, terms such as environment, conservation, ecology, and pollution were not as well known as they are today. Some people had begun to notice the toll big industry was taking on unspoiled American land. Technology and "progress" promised a higher quality of life. Many people believed some sacrifices were necessary to achieve this better lifestyle, but most people did not realize the full extent of the damage on their surroundings, or the harm they were bringing upon themselves.

Rachel's book helped change the way people thought about their environment and natural resources. In her study, Rachel focused on the dangers of large-scale use of pesticides and other chemicals. These poisons were being

▼ A young mother in Brooklyn, New York, sprays DDT in her son's bedroom to kill any insects that may be in the home. Pesticide manufacturers had assured the American people that the pesticides were harmful only to insects.

sprayed on all life forms, including humans, without any knowledge of what might happen over time. No one had seriously considered the possible long-term effects of such use.

The Public Pays the Big Price

Pesticides were big business. Chemical manufacturers were making huge profits, and some government agencies were supporting them. Yet, as Rachel stated on television, "It is the public that is being asked to assume the risks that the insect controllers calculate. The public must decide whether it wishes to continue on the present road, and it can only do so when in full possession of the facts."

Contrary to what her opponents said, Rachel was not completely opposed to the use of chemical sprays. Rather, she wanted them to be used wisely and with great care, and only in times of necessity. They should not be used to exterminate entire species or for mere convenience.

GOD BLESS MOMMA... AND POPPA... AND RACHEL CARSON!

Thank You, Rachel!
The public's reaction to *Silent Spring* took several forms. Many people talked about the issues with each other. Newspapers and magazines published articles and reader editorials. Television news people reported and filmed the different points of view they were hearing around the country. Cartoons also played a role in this discussion. Many, such as the one shown above, expressed opinions about Rachel's work in powerfully visual ways.

◄ The United States government eventually banned the use of DDT. Many bird species that were threatened by pesticides began to regain their place in nature. This beautiful, healthy family of peregrine falcons may not have existed with the continued use of DDT.

Chapter 2

Growing Up in Pennsylvania

Rachel Louise Carson was born in Springdale, Pennsylvania, on May 27, 1907. The large steel town of Pittsburgh was about 15 miles (24 km) away. The Carson family owned a 65-acre (26-hectare) farm set on a hill just outside Springdale that overlooked the Allegheny River. The land was lush and unspoiled by the heavy industry that was moving across America at that time. The natural beauty of the land was a sanctuary for the Carsons as they struggled to make a living during difficult economic times.

Rachel's Family

Robert Warden Carson, Rachel's father, had dreams of making his fortune in real estate. He bought the family farm with the hope of selling parts of it and making a good profit. In the meantime, he had apple and pear orchards to bring in a little money. He also had chickens and a few other farm animals. When he realized the land was not going to sell as he had hoped, Mr. Carson sold insurance. He also worked at the West Penn Power Plant in Springdale.

▲ Rachel Carson as a young girl. She was a quiet child who learned to admire the beauty of nature at an early age.

Maria McLean Carson, Rachel's mother, first met Robert Carson when his church vocal group performed in her hometown of Washington, Pennsylvania. Maria was a young schoolteacher at the time. She also sang and played piano as a member of the Washington Quintette Club. Robert and Maria married in 1894 and moved to Springdale a few years later. Maria had to stop teaching after she married. Married women of that time were expected to remain at home and raise a family. In addition to caring for her home and family, Maria tended a large vegetable garden, sold produce from the farm in town, and gave piano lessons out of the family home.

Rachel was the youngest of three children. Her sister Marian was ten years older, and her brother Robert was eight years older than she was. Although the children were several years apart, the family was close. While the older children attended school, Mrs. Carson focused her attention on Rachel.

"If a child is to keep alive his inborn sense of wonder. . .he needs the companionship of at least one adult who can share it, rediscovering with him the joy, excitement and mystery of the world we live in."

- from Rachel's book
The Sense of Wonder

▲ The Carson family home in Springdale, Pennsylvania.

◀ Rachel's family lived along the beautiful Allegheny River, which runs through the states of New York and Pennsylvania.

Rufous-sided Towhee

Eastern Bluebird

Gray Catbird

Days for the Carson family were busy with work and school, and everyone also had to help with the farm chores. In the evenings, the family spent most of their free time together. Sometimes they gathered to sing favorite songs, with Mrs. Carson playing the piano. Other times they played games or discussed world events, and Mrs. Carson often read to her children.

A Love for the Sea

Marian, Robert, and Rachel loved hearing their mother read aloud. Maria Carson read beautifully. Although Maria read books on various subjects, many of Rachel's favorite stories and poems were about the sea. She had never seen the sea, but she enjoyed the thrilling poems and tales of writers such as John Masefield and Robert Louis Stevenson. Even before she saw the sea for the first time, Rachel

▶ ▲ Maria Carson (shown at right with her three children) spent many hours outdoors with her young daughter. She taught Rachel to recognize the different birds and other creatures that lived around their home (above). Rachel could identify birds by their colors and their songs.

dreamed about its beautiful, powerful, presence. She felt a strong pull to the sea, its tides, and the wealth of life that existed in its vast waters.

As a very young child, Rachel learned to appreciate nature. Mrs. Carson took her daughter on long walks during the day or while the other children were doing homework or late-afternoon chores. Together, mother and daughter explored the farm's varied landscape, including the wooded areas, clear streams, and open fields. Mrs. Carson taught Rachel to look and listen carefully to all the sights and sounds of nature. Rachel was soon able to identify different birds and their songs. She learned about insects and other animals, the incredible variety of plant life, and the twinkling wonders in the night sky.

The Wonder of Nature

Rachel had wonderful memories about the time she spent as a child exploring nature with her mother. In fact, she and Maria Carson spent most of their lives together. Mrs. Carson felt from the beginning that Rachel would be able to achieve much in life. She wanted to make sure her daughter had every opportunity possible.

Maria also encouraged Rachel from an early age to explore Earth's beauty and to respect all forms of life. As an adult, Rachel remembered these times with her mother and wished every child could have such experiences. She also hoped that every child could grow up to realize how much nature was a part of human life. In her book *The Sense of Wonder*, Rachel encourages adults to spend time with their children in nature.

◀ Rachel talks to a young, and eager, audience about the mystery and beauty of nature. She met these boys in the woods near her summer cottage in Maine.

13

A Reverence for All Life

Mrs. Carson also explained that nature had its own ways of developing and surviving. She believed humans should respect all living things. If insects appeared in the Carson home, Maria would catch them and return them outdoors. This reverence for all life became a part of Rachel's own beliefs. Although she spent a lot of time alone as a child, she was never bored. She was happy playing in nature with her pets and the incredible little creatures she discovered.

Rachel attended Springdale Elementary School when she was six. She was an excellent student, but she did not make friends easily.

Rachel had spent most of her young life alone on the farm with her family, and she was shy and quiet. She got along well with everyone, but didn't want to be the center of attention. She concentrated on her schoolwork.

Mrs. Carson was very protective of Rachel's health. She had scarlet fever before attending first grade, and her mother did not believe her daughter was very strong as a result of that illness. She kept Rachel home from school much of the time because she did not want her to catch any colds or other childhood diseases.

Missing so much school did not help Rachel make new friends, but Mrs. Carson educated her daughter very well at home. As a former teacher, she expected a lot from Rachel and made

▼ A United States Army Air Service poster. Rachel's brother Robert enlisted in this branch of the military during World War I.

homeschooling every bit as challenging as the elementary school. Even though Rachel sometimes missed as much as a month of school at a time, she always caught up quickly and made good grades when she returned to the classroom.

Marian married when Rachel was nine. The next year, in 1917, the U.S. entered World War I, and Rachel's brother Robert joined the United States Army Air Service. The entire family, like the rest of the country, was concerned about the war. They anxiously awaited news about what was happening from the many letters Robert wrote home.

During this time, Rachel read *St. Nicholas*, a popular children's magazine designed for readers from ages five to 18. The magazine offered quality

▲ Rachel's favorite writers respected nature, as she did. They also believed that humans should protect their environment and all forms of life. One of these writers, Beatrix Potter, wrote tales about animals that had many human qualities. Potter was also a conservationist and a farmer, and she devoted much of her life to the preservation of unspoiled farmland and the wildlife that it harbored.

Favorite Nature Writers
In addition to reading her favorite magazines, Rachel enjoyed reading "The Tale of Peter Rabbit" and other animal stories by Beatrix Potter, and Kenneth Grahame's "The Wind in the Willows." As she grew older, Rachel read many books about the natural world. A few of her favorite authors were Henry David Thoreau, Ernest Thompson Seton, John Muir, and John Burroughs. One of her favorite books was *Tarka the Otter,* by Henry Williamson. The story of heroic little Tarka was written from the otter's point of view. This approach to writing appealed to Rachel. Much later, when she wrote her first book, *Under the Sea Wind*, she also wrote through the experiences of the animals in and around the sea. In a letter to a friend, Rachel said, "[Henry Williamson] has influenced my writing more than anyone else, and to link my book with his is the greatest tribute you could possibly give it."

St. Nicholas Magazine

St. Nicholas Magazine for young readers was published from 1873–1941. It featured the work of the best writers and illustrators of the time. Rachel eagerly awaited each new issue.

In 1918, Rachel submitted a story she had written called "A Battle in the Clouds." In this story, the enemy blew up part of a plane's wings. Instead of just giving up and crashing to Earth, the young pilot left his comrade in the plane, climbed out of the cockpit, and slowly crawled to the edge of the damaged wing. He eased himself down, held on tight with both hands, and used his body to balance the plane until it landed safely. Enemy pilots could have fired on him at any time, but they were so impressed with his courage they allowed him to land safely.

writing and illustrations on various subjects. Rachel enjoyed the entire magazine, but her favorite articles and stories were those about the natural world. All readers were invited to submit original written pieces to the magazine. If accepted, those pieces were published in the magazine, under a special section called the "St. Nicholas League."

A Writer Is Born

Rachel loved to read. She believed that because she enjoyed stories so much, she should try writing one herself. Her brother wrote a letter about a brave Canadian war pilot who was part of a plane fight in the sky. This thrilling account was just the right material for a story. Rachel decided to write one and send it to *St. Nicholas* when she was ten. The magazine published "A Battle in the Clouds" in the "St. Nicholas League" in September of 1918. She was awarded a silver badge for the story and gained membership to the League. Rachel was proud of her story and continued writing.

▶ *St. Nicholas* magazine offered young readers good writing and illustrations that encouraged them to notice their natural surroundings as well as what was happening in the world. The top headline of this issue's cover states: "When you finish this magazine, place a 1-cent stamp on this notice, mail the magazine, and it will be placed in the hands of our soldiers or sailors destined to proceed overseas."

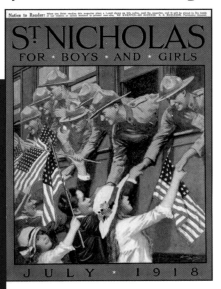

The magazine published two more of her stories within the next year. Rachel decided then that she would work even harder at school so that one day she could make her living as a writer.

Working to Fulfill a Dream

Maria Carson was proud of her daughter. She also worked harder to see that Rachel had the chance to fulfill her dream. Rachel continued to excel in all her subjects. After completing elementary school, she attended high school in Springdale, but Springdale High School was only a two-year school. Many students stopped their education at this point, but Rachel wanted to graduate with four years so she could go to college after graduation. She spent her last two high school years at Parnassus High School in nearby Kensington. Rachel rode the streetcar to school and back each day. She graduated first in her class in 1925.

Yet Rachel did not study so hard just to go to college. She also was naturally curious about the world and wanted to learn all she could. In her free time, Rachel enjoyed walking and exploring on her family's land. As she said later as an adult, "I can remember no time when I wasn't interested in the out-of-doors and the whole world of nature." To Rachel, the natural world was fascinating and peaceful and always full of surprises.

"Rachel's like the mid-day Sun
Always very bright
Never stops her studying
'Till she gets it right."

- A rhyme written by Rachel's classmates and printed next to her high school yearbook photo.

▼ A friend took this photograph of Rachel sitting on a mountaintop in the 1960s. She enjoyed the beauty of the countryside, using binoculars to see details up close.

Chapter 3

In 1925, Rachel entered Pennsylvania College for Women in Pittsburgh (now Chatham College). She wanted to be a writer and was ready to begin her studies. Her family did not have much money, but the college offered a small scholarship to help with expenses. Her parents also contributed what they could, but this still was not enough. The president of the college believed in Rachel's ability. She asked private sponsors to pay the rest of Rachel's tuition.

A Promising Student

Making friends was still difficult for Rachel. She didn't have expensive clothes or extra money for social gatherings or trips to the movies. Also, Maria Carson spent nearly every weekend with her daughter. Rachel's classmates, however, came to respect her abilities as a student.

Grace Croff taught freshman English at the college. She recognized Rachel's talent and encouraged her to write for the school newspaper and its literary magazine. Miss Croff was impressed by Rachel's determination to be a writer.

Rachel's first short story in the magazine was titled "The Master of the Ship's Light." Rachel had never seen the sea, yet she wrote clearly and beautifully about its sounds and

▲ Poems and stories about the sea fascinated Rachel as a child, even though she lived far away from the coast and had never seen such a vast body of water. When she finally saw the sea for the first time at age 22, she was overwhelmed by its majesty. She felt that the sea was part of her destiny and wanted to learn all she could about it.

motions. She relied on what she'd heard, read, and imagined. This story was just the beginning for Rachel. In the future, she would write entire books about the sea.

By the end of her first year, Rachel felt that she was on her way to achieving her goals. She did well in her coursework and had even learned how to play the violin in music class. Her second year became a turning point in her education and her future. Rachel was required to take science classes to earn her degree. She loved nature but had not enjoyed science in high school. She signed up for a class in biology.

Mary Scott Skinker was Rachel's biology professor. Miss Skinker was an outstanding teacher who made science exciting. She took her classes on outdoor field trips, where the students could see nature up close. Even the classroom and lab work were fun. These classes stirred Rachel's interest. She thought of herself as a writer, but Miss Skinker's classes made Rachel wonder if science should be her

"I can still remember my intense emotional response as that line spoke to something within me, seeming to tell me that my own path led to the sea— which then I had never seen—and that my own destiny was somehow linked with the sea."

- Rachel, on remembering the life-changing moment when reading Tennyson's poem "Locksley Hall"

◀ Although Mrs. Carson visited during most of Rachel's free time at the college, Rachel was able to spend a little more time with her classmates when she joined the field hockey and basketball teams. In this photo, she is shown standing, second from the right.

▲ Mary Skinker was a science professor at Pennsylvania College for Women. She was a strong, guiding influence for Rachel at the college, and they remained friends for life.

▼ Rachel's mother spent almost every weekend at the college. In this photo, both parents visited their daughter on campus.

chosen field. Rachel had always been fascinated by the natural world. She hoped that someday she could express her passion for this subject in a way that would interest others.

A Double Gift

Rachel found herself in a dilemma. Should she continue her studies to be a writer? Or should she change her plans and become a scientist? At that time, most school programs considered the arts and the sciences to be separate areas of study. Not many people believed one person could be gifted in both areas. Rachel had to choose.

Making such an important decision was difficult. Grace Croff had worked closely with Rachel to develop her writing and boost her confidence. Maria Carson also firmly supported Rachel's plan to become a writer. A change to science would be difficult for her to understand. Yet, Mary Skinker's extraordinary classes had awakened a new area of Rachel's abilities. She began to realize that writing poems and stories would not be the full story of her life.

One particularly stormy evening, Rachel sat alone reading a poem titled "Locksley Hall." The poem was written by Alfred, Lord Tennyson and was part of an assignment for Grace Croff's English class. As the wind howled outdoors, shaking the windows of her room, Rachel read these final lines and felt that her life was about to change:

> *Let it fall on Locksley Hall, with rain or hail or fire or snow;*
> *For the mighty wind arises, roaring seaward, and I go.*

A Moment of Clarity

The final line, especially, seemed to be giving Rachel guidance. Rachel's future took on a new clarity. She changed her major from English to biology.

Rachel's decision did not receive much support at first. The other girls at school thought she was making a mistake because she was such a good writer. The college president, as well as Maria Carson, felt Rachel would have more career options as a writer than she would as a scientist. The best career opportunity in science would probably be as a teacher. Rachel thought of Mary Skinker and believed she could make a difference as a teacher, too.

Mary Skinker had become a friend as well as a teacher to Rachel, but Miss Skinker announced that she was leaving the college to complete her doctorate degree at Johns Hopkins University in Baltimore, Maryland. Rachel was disappointed to be losing her mentor, but Mary Skinker kept in touch and suggested that Rachel continue studying to earn a master's degree. Rachel graduated with honors from Pennsylvania College for Women in 1929.

Rachel had applied to Johns Hopkins for graduate school during her senior year at the college. The university offered her a full scholarship toward a degree in marine

▼ Although Rachel had to choose either English or science as a major in college, she eventually found work that allowed her to combine these two great interests. She became both a scientist and a writer.

Catfish Research

Rachel enjoyed being a graduate student at Johns Hopkins University. Her master's thesis was an in-depth study of catfish embryos and the early development of a temporary "head kidney." Also called a "pronephros," this organ formed at the fertilized egg stage and remained until a true kidney formed nearer the tail in the adult catfish. Rachel spent many hours in the university laboratory, dissecting catfish and studying tiny embryos under microscopes. At one point, she wrote to a former classmate from the Pennsylvania College for Women, "The professors are splendid to work with, and the students are a dandy crowd . . . [but] the lab is my world and is going to be my chief existence until I get my degree."

Rachel's professors praised her work and told her she had provided a contribution to science. The writing in her thesis, however, was dry and scholarly. It did not resemble the passionate, poetic qualities of her future writing about the sea.

zoology. She believed at the time that she was giving up a career in writing. Those who knew her best guessed that Rachel would not be able to abandon it entirely.

A Magical Summer at Woods Hole

Before moving to Baltimore, Rachel took advantage of another offer. She spent six weeks at the Marine Biology Laboratory in Woods Hole, Massachusetts. Woods Hole was an ocean research center. It was here that Rachel finally got her first look at the sea. Working at the center was a great adventure. She met famous scientists and made friends who shared her interest in the natural world, and the sea in particular. The beauty and majesty of the ocean were, at times, overwhelming. It was more magical than she had imagined. She worked right on the water's edge, observing sea life as it moved and breathed. Again, Rachel felt her world opening up to new possibilities.

▲ Rachel worked on two other scientific projects before focusing on a study of catfish for her master's thesis. Her final paper helped her earn a degree as a marine zoologist.

◀ Rachel on a boat at the Woods Hole Oceanic Research Center in Massachusetts in 1929. Although she visited the center for research purposes later in her career, she would always remember the excitement of her first summer there.

On her way to Johns Hopkins University, Rachel visited the United States Bureau of Fisheries in Washington, D.C. Elmer Higgins was a supervisor at the bureau. Rachel talked to Mr. Higgins about her plans to become a scientist and asked his advice about the possibility of future jobs. Elmer Higgins was honest. He told Rachel the bureau had never hired a female scientist and that she should concentrate on becoming a teacher. Still, he was impressed by Rachel's manner and quiet determination. He told her to visit him again once she had a graduate degree.

The Crash

Rachel's life at Johns Hopkins was devoted to classes, study, and research. Only a few weeks after the first semester began, the United States Stock Market crashed. People all across the country lost their jobs and had no way to make a living or feed

► The Great Depression affected everyone in the United States. People everywhere lost their jobs and had to live on whatever they could earn doing small odd jobs and growing their own food when possible. Many families had to leave their homes and travel around the country looking for a way to make a living.

Feline Friends

Rachel and Maria Carson loved cats. They were independent yet devoted companions in the Carson home.

In one letter to a Cat Welfare Association, Rachel said that the cats in her home helped her write books. Buzzie and Kito held papers in place and kept her company for *Under the Sea Wind*. Tippy did the same for *The Sea Around Us,* and Muffie and Jeffie for *The Edge of the Sea*. The cats were wonderful friends for a writer who spent much time alone.

their families. Businesses failed and banks closed their doors. It seemed as if the entire country had come to a screeching halt. The Great Depression had begun.

Even with a full scholarship, Rachel had to take on two part-time jobs in addition to her studies. Her parents were having financial difficulties in Springdale, so she invited them to live with her in a small rented house in Baltimore. Mrs. Carson did the housework, and Mr. Carson found small jobs in the city. Rachel's sister Marian also moved in a few months later with her two young daughters, Virginia and Marjorie. Rachel's brother Robert joined them, too, the following year. He did whatever work he could find and helped pay for food. One time an employer paid Robert partly in cash, and gave him a cat and her kittens as the rest. Mitzi and the kittens made everyone laugh with their antics, and Rachel had yet another connection to the natural world.

◄ Rachel working at home with the help of her cat Moppet in 1962.

Chapter 4

A Huge Push Forward

Rachel completed her master's degree at Johns Hopkins in 1932. She intended to continue her studies and earn a doctorate, but family problems and a lack of money forced her to change plans. Robert had moved out of the house, and Marian was ill with diabetes. Rachel had to find full-time work.

Hard Times

In 1935, Mr. Carson died unexpectedly of a heart attack. The family sent his body to Pennsylvania, where his sisters took care of the burial. Rachel and her mother could not afford to attend the services.

Rachel now had the full responsibility of caring for Mrs. Carson, Marian, and the two girls, as well as herself. She paid a second visit to Elmer Higgins at the Bureau of Fisheries. The bureau sponsored a radio program titled "Romance Under the Waters," which the staff jokingly called "Seven-Minute Fish Tales." Mr. Higgins was having trouble finding someone who knew science and could also write. He offered Rachel a part-time job writing the radio scripts.

Although she enjoyed her work at the bureau, Rachel needed more than part-time work to support her family. She took a

▲ Spraying pesticides to kill insects affects other animal life. For example, caddisflies live in and near streams and cold-water rivers. These insects are a source of food for salmon and other fish. When pesticides kill the caddisflies, the food supply is gone, and the number of fish decrease.

United States Civil Service examination. The only woman to take the exam, Rachel had the highest score and was offered a job as junior aquatic biologist. She was now a full-time member of Mr. Higgins' staff. Her work would be primarily as a science writer.

A Compliment . . . of Sorts

Once the radio broadcasts were complete, Rachel worked on pamphlets about sea life. The department decided to combine the pamphlets into a booklet, and Mr. Higgins asked Rachel to write the introduction. She worked all day and night on the assignment and handed in several pages the next day. Mr. Higgins read the introduction but told Rachel he couldn't use it. He felt the writing was "too good" for the booklet. He said she should write another introduction and send her original version to the *Atlantic Monthly*, a leading literary magazine.

In early 1937, Marian died suddenly of pneumonia. She left behind her two young daughters. Rachel and her mother decided to take responsibility for Virginia and Marjorie. Rachel also moved the family into a new home in Silver Spring, Maryland, a suburb of Washington, D.C. This house was much closer to the bureau.

To earn extra money, Rachel wrote even more. She sent her first introduction to the bureau's sea booklet to the *Atlantic Monthly*. The magazine published the essay "Undersea" in its September 1937 issue. It was Rachel's first nationally published article. Readers enjoyed the subject as well as Rachel's clear, expressive writing style.

▲ Rachel Carson's devotion to her work as a writer and a scientist—along with her passion for the sea—combined to help her through good times and bad.

Mr. Higgins read the article and told Rachel she should write an entire book about life in the sea. Other experts agreed. Rachel loved writing, but she worked full-time at the bureau and needed to spend time with her young nieces. How could she work on a book? Her solution was to write in the evenings and on the weekends, late into the night. Her cats kept her company. During the day, Mrs. Carson would type a clean copy of the manuscript with changes from the night before.

Success—and Then War

Under the Sea-Wind reached bookstores in early November 1941. Rachel said the book ". . . was written to make the sea and its life as vivid a reality for those who may read the book as it has become for me during the past decade."

Rachel wanted her readers to "experience" life in the sea as much as possible, and to see how different species interacted and depended on each other as they lived out their lives. To accomplish this, she made the sea the central focus of the book. She also followed the life cycles of sea animals from their individual points of view. Rynchops the skimmer, Scomber the mackerel, and Anguilla the eel were only three of the many characters that made the sea come alive for Rachel's readers. The book immediately received excellent reviews.

Rachel could not enjoy the attention for long. Japan bombed

▲ Rachel wanted readers of *Under the Sea-Wind* to get an accurate picture of life in and around the sea. She gave some of the sea animals—such as the skimmer, mackerel, and eel shown here—names and characteristics that readers could understand. She also explained how the animals interacted with each other and their environment.

The United States Fish and Wildlife Service works to conserve and protect wildlife and its habitats. It also publishes information booklets for the public. Rachel worked on several projects during her career there.

Pearl Harbor in Hawaii on December 7, 1941, and the United States entered World War II. The war effort changed people's lives in many ways. Little money was available for books. The timing was unfortunate. Although the book did not sell very well, Rachel continued to receive encouraging reviews from other scientists.

In 1940, the Bureau of Fisheries was renamed the Fish and Wildlife Service. It was now part of the United States Department of the Interior. One of Rachel's assignments during the war was to write pamphlets that encouraged people to eat more fish and other types of seafood. Food was rationed during the war. Many people, especially those who did not live near water, needed to find new sources of protein.

At work, Rachel began to read reports about chemical use during the war. A pesticide called DDT was sprayed on soldiers overseas to kill insects that carried disease. Rachel was concerned that the use of this chemical was not being monitored for long-term effects. What would be the end result of the spraying—for humans and the rest of nature?

Pursuing a Literary Career

The quality of Rachel's work earned her several promotions. She eventually became Biologist and Editor-in-Chief for the Fish and Wildlife Service. One of the projects Rachel coordinated was Conservation in Action. Twelve booklets introduced people to the country's wildlife sanctuaries. Rachel also used the project to

◀ Protecting the environment and all forms of life on Earth was a life mission for Rachel Carson. She dedicated her time to writing books that both delighted and informed people of the many wonders of nature. She also encouraged readers to actively conserve the world's precious natural resources. To honor her efforts, the Rachel Carson National Wildlife Refuge was dedicated in 1970 near Rachel's cottage in Maine.

encourage people to conserve the country's natural resources. As she explained, "We in the United States have been slow to learn that our wildlife, like other forms of natural wealth, must be vigorously protected if we are to continue to enjoy its benefits."

Although her first book had not sold many copies, Rachel decided to write a second one. In this book, she wrote about the sea from the time of its earliest formation to the present. She described the history and physical features of Earth's seas, the movements of the water, and the plant and animal life forms that developed and evolved in the watery environment. She also explored humankind's relationship to the sea. She presented the sea as a precious natural resource that must be protected.

Rachel hired a literary agent named Marie Rodell to help find a publisher. Marie was an excellent agent. A friendship as well as a partnership quickly developed between the two women. Marie worked with Rachel throughout her writing career.

"We live in a scientific age; yet we assume that knowledge of science is the prerogative of only a small number of human beings, isolated and priestlike in their laboratories. This is not true. The materials of science are the materials of life itself."

- from Rachel's acceptance speech for the National Book Award for Non-Fiction in 1952 for *The Sea Around Us*

Rachel spent long hours at work but wrote late at night and on weekends again. As with the first book, Mrs. Carson typed clean manuscripts for Rachel during the day. Rachel talked to many scientists and other sea experts. She went on a deep-sea diving expedition and other trips to gather information. She also won a fellowship that allowed her to take a leave of absence from work. For a short while, she was able to write full-time.

A Huge Hit

Published in July of 1951, *The Sea Around Us* was an instant success. Rachel became famous almost overnight. By August, the book was a *New York Times* best seller. The public loved the book, and Rachel received several professional awards for her accomplishment. Her passion for the sea came through in her scientific, yet poetic, style of writing. More than 250,000 copies of the book sold in the first year.

Following the success of *The Sea Around*

▶ National Book Award winners talk to the master of ceremonies in New York City in 1952. From left to right: Marianne Moore, author of *Collected Poems of Marianne Moore*; James Jones, author of *From Here to Eternity*; and Rachel Carson, author of *The Sea Around Us*.

Us, a new edition of Rachel's first book, *Under the Sea-Wind*, appeared in 1952. The new edition sold extremely well. Rachel had two books on the bestseller list at the same time.

Rachel could now afford to write full-time. She resigned from the Fish and Wildlife Service. She bought land and built a cottage on the coast in West Southport, Maine. She named it Silverledges. Rachel and her family spent many wonderful summers at the shore. They returned to the house in Silver Spring for the rest of each year.

Rachel had two close friends in Maine. Dorothy and Stanley Freeman had a cottage close to hers. The Freemans admired her work and introduced themselves when Rachel first moved to the area. The three became close friends. They enjoyed exploring the coastline, hiking in the forest, reading to one another, and having summer picnics. Dorothy, especially, shared Rachel's fascination with the teeming shore life and wooded land along the Maine coast.

Rachel's third book, *The Edge of the Sea*, was published in 1955. This book described the three different types of shorelines that connect the seas to dry

From Book to Film
The Sea Around Us sold very successfully in book form, and RKO Pictures in Hollywood also produced a documentary based on the book. Studio writers developed the script, which contained many factual errors. Rachel and her agent Marie Rodell spent long hours trying to correct these errors. Although Rachel was not happy with the final version, it won an Oscar award in 1952 for best full-length documentary film.

▲ Rachel's cottage in Maine was a haven for her during the summer months. The area's shoreline teemed with tiny creatures and plant life that engaged Rachel's interest and helped her relax after long months of hard work in Maryland. **31**

Movie Time

Bob Hines was a gifted illustrator who worked with Rachel at the Fish and Wildlife Service. The two were good friends. Bob also worked with Rachel on *The Edge of the Sea*. He drew all the book's illustrations—more than 150. Bob liked to draw from life. While he and Rachel worked on the book, they spent time gathering buckets of sand and seawater containing plants and sea life that existed in tidal pools along the shore. They studied all the little creatures and plants under a microscope. Rachel would quickly write detailed notes about the specimens. Bob would get a clear, close look at his subjects and make accurate sketches. When they had the information they needed, Rachel and Bob would carry the pails back down to the tidal pools, and carefully return the plants and animals to their homes.

land. She described the communities of plants and animals that live along the shore and in the sea, how they came into being, and how they evolved over time. "All the life of the shore—the past and the present—by the very fact of its existence there, gives evidence that it has dealt successfully with the sea itself, and the subtle life relationships that bind each living thing to its community."

The Edge of the Sea, like Rachel's first two books, became a bestseller.

A Child's Touch

One of Rachel's next projects was an article about the value of introducing children to the wonders of nature. She thought of her grandnephew Roger Allen Christie as she wrote this article. Rachel's niece Marjorie and her

▶ Bob Hines puts the finishing touches on a wall-sized depiction of North Carolina's Mattamuskeet National Wildlife Refuge. He was the only artist the United States Fish and Wildlife Service has ever employed.

◄ Rachel and her grandnephew Roger Christie spent many happy hours exploring the coast near her cottage in Maine. Roger brought a child's innocent sense of delight to their discoveries in the natural world.

young son Roger spent a lot of time with Rachel and Maria Carson. Marjorie's health was poor. Rachel helped her niece as much as she could.

From the time he was two, Rachel and Roger explored the outdoors together. He brought a child's happy sense of curiosity to their activities.

The article "Help Your Child to Wonder" was published in *Woman's Home Companion* in 1956. The writing was beautifully personal, and readers loved it. Ten years later, the article appeared in book form filled with photographs taken along the Maine coast and titled *The Sense of Wonder*.

In early 1957, Marjorie, whose health had been frail for some time, died of pneumonia. At the age of five, Roger was alone. By this time, Maria Carson was in her late 80s. She suffered from arthritis and needed constant care. Rachel had developed a special bond with her grandnephew. She decided to formally adopt Roger.

" If I had influence with the good fairy who is supposed to preside over the christening of all children, I should ask that her gift to each child in the world be a sense of wonder so indestructible that it would last throughout life . . . "

- from Rachel's magazine article, "Help Your Child to Wonder"

Chapter 5

Brilliant Controversy and Mission Accomplished

▲ An egret searches for food scraps in a sandy area strewn with garbage. In *Silent Spring*, Rachel urges readers to realize how human carelessness affects Earth's environment and all forms of life.

Rachel had several new writing projects planned, but she also had many family responsibilities. Her mother's health was failing, and Roger needed Rachel's comfort and attention after the death of his own mother. It was difficult to find time to work.

A Plea for Help

In January 1958, Rachel received a letter from a friend named Olga Owens Huckins. Mrs. Huckins owned land in Massachusetts that she and her husband had turned into a bird sanctuary. The land was sprayed with the pesticide DDT to kill mosquitoes. Not long after the spraying, Olga discovered the bodies of several birds on her property. She said the mosquitoes were still there, but other insects had disappeared. She asked Rachel for help.

Olga had sent a letter to the *Boston Herald* about the incident, but she hoped to find people to contact on the government level. The spraying had to stop. Rachel had been concerned about the effects of pesticides for several years. In 1945, she had offered to write an article for *Reader's Digest* on the dangers of pesticide use. The magazine turned her down.

After reading Olga's letter, Rachel began to do serious research on the use of pesticides, especially DDT. Rachel knew about this pesticide from its use in World War II. Her research convinced her to write a book on the dangers of pesticides and other chemicals in use at that time. People needed to know the truth about these poisons.

Marie Rodell helped Rachel find a publisher for her book. Rachel did not know if the American public would buy it. This project was vastly different from her previous books, but she was certain of one thing. A book on this subject would cause trouble with pesticide manufacturers and the agencies that supported them.

New Setbacks at Home

Rachel's life at home had another setback. Maria Carson, the strongest influence in Rachel's life, died in December 1958. Rachel spent many hours beside her mother's bed, holding Maria's hand until Mrs. Carson slipped away, at the age of 89. Now only Rachel and Roger were left in the Silver Spring house.

Rachel had been having problems with her own health. The early spring of 1960 was especially difficult. She had the flu and a sinus infection. She was diagnosed with arthritis, and developed a stomach ulcer. She also found a lump in her breast. Her surgeon removed a tumor and said she would recover. A few months later, Rachel learned that her doctor had not told her the truth. She had breast

"There is one quality that characterizes all of us who deal with the sciences of the earth and its life—we are never bored. We can't be. There is always something new to be investigated. Every mystery solved brings us to the threshold of a greater one."

\- Rachel Carson

▲ A respected biologist and author, Rachel never lost her sense of curiosity and wonder for the natural world. Here, she tries to capture some of nature's beauty on film while walking in the woods near her cottage in Maine.

DDT

DDT (dichloro-diphenyl-trichloroethane) is a chemical pesticide. In a 1958 letter to the *Boston Herald*, Olga Owens Huckins described damage from the deadly DDT sprayings over her home, in a way that could not be ignored:

"Since we live close to the marshes, we were treated to several lethal doses. . . The 'harmless' shower bath killed several of our lovely songbirds outright. We picked up three dead bodies the next morning right by the door. They were birds that had lived close to us, trusted us, and built their nests in our trees year after year. The next day three were scattered around the birdbath. (I had emptied it and scrubbed it after the spraying but YOU CAN NEVER KILL DDT.)"

DDT poisoning lasts a long time. It builds up in the environment and in plant and animal life. Humans absorb DDT through food and water that has been contaminated. After years of debate and controversy, DDT was banned in the United States in 1972.

cancer. She found a new surgeon in Cleveland, Ohio. He and Rachel agreed on a plan to treat the cancer.

In spite of this news, Rachel continued to care for Roger and work on the book. Olga's story was just one of many shocking accounts about pesticide use. Other people wrote to Rachel about their experiences with the spraying. The poisons were affecting all forms of life, including humans.

Rachel's Groundbreaking Work

Silent Spring was published on September 27, 1962. The book opened with a fable. Rachel described a town that did not really exist, but could be real if change did not occur. The people in the town lived in harmony with nature. Wildlife was plentiful and the land was rich for farming. Then something happened to change this beautiful way of life. The animals and plants began to die. People noticed that even the birds were gone. What had happened? Then someone remembered that a white powder had fallen from the sky a few weeks past. Traces of this pesticide still remained on the land. In Rachel's words: "No witchcraft, no

▶ A private shipyard company tests a new insecticidal fogging machine on a stretch of beach at Jones Island, New York, in 1945. Sadly, young children, the men spraying DDT, all other life forms, and the environment were exposed to this deadly chemical.

enemy action had silenced the rebirth of new life in this stricken world. The people had done it themselves."

Rachel explained that humans were destroying their world. She said that "the most alarming of all man's assaults upon the environment is the contamination of air, earth, rivers, and sea with dangerous and even lethal materials." She wrote in detail about the different pesticides being sprayed in the United States. She described how animals were dying painful deaths from the chemical sprays. Entire species of plant and animal life were being exterminated. Many waterways and the life within them were contaminated.

Rachel explained how pesticides were affecting the human population. Earth, the air, the water, the food supply—everything was becoming contaminated. Humans were getting sick and dying from the poisons, and yet the chemical industries continued to develop newer, more lethal, chemicals.

"The beauty of the living world I was trying to save has always been uppermost in my mind—that, and anger at the senseless, brutish things that were being done. I have felt bound by a solemn obligation to do what I could—if I didn't at least try I could never again be happy in nature. But now I can believe I have at least helped a little."

- from Rachel in a letter to friend Lois Crisler just before the release of *Silent Spring*

◄ Pesticide poisoning threatened the future of brown pelicans in the United States in the 1970s. DDT caused the birds' eggshells to be too thin to support the embryos inside. Since DDT was banned, brown pelicans have managed to slowly regain their population and their place in nature.

37

Awards and Honors

Rachel received many awards for *Silent Spring*. These awards reflected a respect and gratitude for Rachel's entire body of work as well as her deep, personal affection for all forms of life. She received the Schweitzer Medal from the Animal Welfare Institute. The National Wildlife Federation named her Conservationist of the Year. She received medals from the National Audubon Society and the American Geographical Society. Rachel also was elected to the American Academy of Arts and Letters.

Further evidence of the lasting impact of Rachel's work has made its way into the nation's history. On April 22, 1970, Earth Day was organized in the United States to celebrate our planet and to discuss ways to preserve the environment (right). Today, hundreds of millions of people worldwide participate in Earth Day activities.

Rachel wrote *Silent Spring* for two main reasons. The first was to warn the American people about the dangers of pesticides. The second was to encourage the government to regulate the chemical industry. She assured readers that chemicals were not the only way to deal with insect pests. She offered natural, biological alternatives to the insect problems.

To Rachel's surprise, *Silent Spring* made the *New York Times* best seller list after only two weeks. Copies sold as fast as they could be printed. As Rachel predicted, the book provoked a huge controversy. Negative attacks on *Silent Spring* and on Rachel's abilities as a scientist and writer began immediately.

Drawing the Line on Pesticides

Chemical companies and the United States Department of Agriculture were Rachel's loudest critics. Company representatives said Rachel's work was inaccurate. The Department of Agriculture supported the pesticide industry

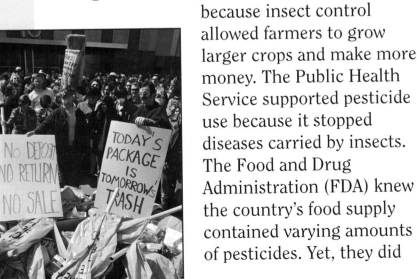

because insect control allowed farmers to grow larger crops and make more money. The Public Health Service supported pesticide use because it stopped diseases carried by insects. The Food and Drug Administration (FDA) knew the country's food supply contained varying amounts of pesticides. Yet, they did not deal with the problem effectively. Even *Time* magazine said Rachel was trying to frighten the public and that her book had many errors.

Rachel's major opponent was Dr. Robert White-Stevens. Dr. White-Stevens worked for a large chemical manufacturer. He defended the use of pesticides and said they improved the quality of life for Americans. He believed that: "If man were to faithfully follow the teachings of Miss Carson, we would return to the Dark Ages, and the insects and diseases and vermin would once again inherit the earth."

At a press conference in the summer of 1962, reporters asked President John F. Kennedy about the pesticide issue. The president said he was concerned, especially since the publication of *Silent Spring*. He set up a special committee to study all the facts. The committee's report a few months later criticized the chemical industry, the Department of Agriculture, and the FDA. The committee also publicly recognized the importance of *Silent Spring*.

"A Scientist and a Poet of Nature"

On April 3, 1963, CBS News aired "The Silent Spring of Rachel Carson." Eric Sevareid, the program moderator, knew Rachel was very ill, but she wanted the chance to speak to the American people. Mr. Sevareid brought the camera crew to her home to film the interview.

▲ A farmer sits among the chemicals he uses on his large farm. The amount of chemicals shown here would last about one year. At that time, pesticides were used to kill insect pests that might threaten his crop, and synthetic fertilizers boosted the soil's ability to produce more abundant crops. By using these toxic chemicals, the farmer's animals, as well as the crops he produced, were all infected with various levels of poisons. The produce and many of the animals were then sold at market to people around the country. **39**

Role Model and Inspiration

Rachel Carson's life and work have influenced many generations of readers. Today, thousands of groups and millions of people worldwide are deeply committed to protecting and conserving Earth and its various forms of life.

In 1994, United States Vice President Al Gore wrote the introduction to a new printing of *Silent Spring*. Mr. Gore praised Rachel's science and writing, her personal courage in the face of strong opposition, and her vision for Earth's future. A dedicated environmentalist and author of two books in the field, Mr. Gore remembers being greatly moved by Rachel's book. He stated: "*Silent Spring* came as a cry in the wilderness, a deeply felt, thoroughly researched, and brilliantly written argument that changed the course of history. Without this book, the environmental movement might have been long delayed or never have developed at all."

He later described Rachel as "a scientist and a poet of nature." Mr. Sevareid also interviewed Dr. Robert White-Stevens, the United States Secretary of Agriculture, the chief of the Public Health Service, and the commissioner of the FDA for the program. Rachel's interview convinced even more of the American public that she was correct.

In June, Rachel appeared before a Senate sub-committee. The committee members wanted to hear her opinions about pollution and the environment. Rachel also spoke about the dangers of pesticides and other chemical poisons. She said ordinary people had been subjected to pesticides, and many had become ill because of the spraying.

Exhausted from all the work and attention, Rachel left for her Maine cottage in the summer of 1963. Roger, who was now 11 years of age, and the two cats went with her. She did not know it at the time, but this trip would be

▲ In June 1963, Rachel testified before a special Senate sub-committee. Committee members wanted to know her opinions about the dangers of using pesticides and how other types of pollution could affect people and the environment.

Rachel's last summer near her beloved sea. Too ill to climb the rocky ledges at the cottage, she spent quiet time looking through her microscope at tiny tidal pool creatures everyone brought to her. She cooked and read, and spent valuable time with Roger and the Freemans. She even found time to write a little.

In early fall, despite her fragile health, Rachel traveled to California. She had always wanted to see the redwood trees. Marie Rodell went with her. Rachel first gave a lecture in San Francisco. Afterward, in a wheelchair, she visited beautiful Muir Woods.

A Full Life and Lasting Legacy

Although she remained optimistic about the amount of time she had left, Rachel's health continued to decline. On April 14, 1964, Rachel Louise Carson died at her home in Silver Spring, Maryland. She was 56 years old.

Rachel had lived a full life in a short amount of time. She cared deeply for her family and

Awards and Honors
The awards and honors continued after Rachel's death. In 1980, President Jimmy Carter posthumously awarded Rachel the Presidential Medal of Freedom. Her grandnephew, Roger Christie, accepted the award on Rachel's behalf. In 1981, the United States Postal Service issued a Rachel Carson stamp in her honor. In 1999, *Time* magazine listed Rachel Carson as one of the "Top 20 Most Influential Scientists and Thinkers of the 20th Century."

▲ Rachel enjoys the beauty of the outdoors in 1962. Here she hopes to catch glimpses of the many bird species in the area.

▲ Although very fragile, Rachel was able to fulfill one of her life's dreams in fall of 1963 by visiting Muir Woods in California.

Doing Our Part

Everyone can work to keep the environment safe and to conserve natural resources. Here are a few ways you and your family can help:

- Avoid using aerosol or liquid chemical pesticides.
- Recycle whenever you can.
- Reduce the amount of garbage you send to a landfill by starting a compost pile or bin.
- Grow a vegetable garden. This will ensure the safety of your food and save energy.
- Plant trees. They help keep the air clean.
- Use a push mower instead of one that runs on gasoline or electricity.
- Ride a bike or walk for errands and other short trips.
- Shut off lights and appliances when you leave a room.
- Use natural cleaning products.
- Use reusable bags to carry groceries or other purchases instead of asking for plastic or paper bags.
- Cut back on heating and air conditioning use when possible.
- Conserve water.

friends. She celebrated the beauty of the natural world, did all she could to protect Earth's environment, and challenged others to do the same. Rachel always had a new idea, and a new writing project, waiting to be developed.

Rachel left an impressive legacy. Her fascinating books about the sea still interest readers and encourage them to explore their surroundings. *Silent Spring* inspires people from all walks of life to accept her challenge to protect the environment and all life on Earth.

In 1970, the United States government formed the Environmental Protection Agency (EPA). One of the agency's responsibilities is to monitor and regulate pesticides and other toxic chemicals. In 1972, the EPA banned the spraying of DDT in the United States.

Rachel began a revolution when she informed the American public about the dangers of pesticides and other chemical substances. She devoted her adult life to educating others about the connection of all living things. As a result of Rachel's tireless efforts, the United States, as well as the rest of the world, began a heated discussion about the protection of life and Earth's environment that continues today. Rachel Carson accomplished her mission.

▶ A healthy, organic wheat crop grows in close harmony with area wildlife. Rachel Carson's life and work reminded people to enjoy nature, protect all forms of life, and preserve Earth's ecological balance.

Chronology

1907	Rachel Louise Carson is born May 27 in Springdale, Pennsylvania
1918	First published story, "A Battle in the Clouds," appears in *St. Nicholas* magazine
1925	Graduates from high school
1925–1929	Attends the Pennsylvania College for Women; earns a bachelor's degree in biology
1929	Spends summer on a fellowship at the United States Marine Laboratory in Woods Hole, Massachusetts
1929–1932	Studies at Johns Hopkins University; earns a master's degree in marine zoology
1935	Robert Carson, Rachel's father, dies
1936	Works part-time writing radio scripts for the United States Bureau of Fisheries
1936	Takes Civil Service Exam; earns full-time position as junior aquatic biologist with Bureau of Fisheries
1937	Rachel's sister Marian dies
1941	First book, *Under the Sea-Wind*, is published
1951	Second book, *The Sea Around Us,* is published
1955	Third book, *The Edge of the Sea*, is published
1956	Article "Help Your Child to Wonder" is published in *Woman's Home Companion*. (Later published in book form in 1965)
1957	Rachel's niece Marjorie dies. Rachel adopts Roger Allen Christie
1958	Maria Carson, Rachel's mother, dies
1960	Rachel is diagnosed with cancer; begins treatment
1962	Fourth book, *Silent Spring*, is published. A huge controversy results
1963	CBS News presents "The Silent Spring of Rachel Carson" on April 3
1963	Testifies before a Senate sub-committee on environmental hazards
1964	Rachel Carson dies of cancer on April 14
1970	Rachel Carson National Wildlife Refuge is dedicated near her cottage in Maine
1980	Posthumously awarded the Presidential Medal of Freedom by President Jimmy Carter
1981	United States Postal Service issues Rachel Carson stamp
1999	Named one of *Time* magazine's Top 20 Most Influential Scientists and Thinkers of the 20th Century

Glossary

aerosol A spray, such as an insecticide or a medicine, that comes in a pressurized can or other type of container

alarmist A person who causes others to become excited or frightened about something for no apparent reason

comrade A companion, usually as a member of an organization or as a soldier or some other member of a fighting unit

conservation The careful preservation and protection of something, such as a natural resource

contaminate To spoil or make unfit for use

controversial Causing an argument or debate because of opposing opinions

documentary A film that presents facts and information instead of a telling a fictional story

ecology The study of plants and animals and their relationship to their environments

embryo An animal in the very earliest stages of development

environment Everything that surrounds a plant or animal, such as physical landscape, food supply, and climate

exterminate To get rid of completely; to kill off

fable A story that is used to send an important message

fellowship An award of money given to someone for study or research

Great Depression A time during the 1930s in the United States and other nations when many people lost their jobs and businesses lost money

infinite Endless; without boundaries or limits

leave of absence The time when a person has permission to be away from his or her job for a designated period of time

legacy Something that is left behind for future generations

literary agent A person who represents writers in their business dealings with publishers

major The subject in which a college student concentrates, taking more courses in this field than any others

marine biologist A scientist who studies life in the sea

mentor Someone who provides guidance or advice

moderator A person who is in charge of a discussion or debate

natural resources Materials found in nature, such as soil, water, and minerals that people can use

naturalist A person who studies plants and animals where they live in nature

organism Any living thing that can function, or learn to function, on its own

pesticide A substance, usually a chemical poison, used to kill insects and other pests

pollution Substances that make areas of the environment dirty or harmful

prerogative A right or privilege

recycle To use something again; to alter something so that it can be used again

sanctuary A safe or protected place

scholarship A grant or payment made to a student, based on academic performance, financial need, or some other reason

testimony Evidence; information given by a witness

thesis An original study in the form of a long essay or research project

tribute A gift, speech, or other sign of appreciation or respect

tuition The amount of money needed to attend a school or university

zoology The branch of science that deals with the study of animal life

Further Information

Books

Bruchac, Joseph, and Thomas Locker. *Rachel Carson: Preserving a Sense of Wonder*. Fulcrum Publishing, 2009.

Landau, Elaine. *Rachel Carson and the Environmental Movement* (Cornerstones of Freedom). Children's Press, 2004.

Levine, Ellen. *Up Close: Rachel Carson*. Viking, 2007.

Quaratiello, Arlene R. *Rachel Carson: A Biography*. Greenwood Press, 2004.

Web sites

www.rachelcarson.org
This is the official Carson Web site, offering detailed information, images, and resources.

www.fws.gov/rachelcarson/
This is the United States Fish and Wildlife Service site section devoted to Rachel Carson. It offers information and short videos on a variety of subjects linked to Rachel and the Rachel Carson National Wildlife Refuge.

www.fws.gov/northeast/rachelcarson/
The United States Fish and Wildlife Service site on the protected marshlands and estuaries near Rachel Carson's cottage in Maine covers the history of the refuge, brochures, special event information, a biography of Rachel, and more.

www.rachelcarsonhomestead.org/
This site provides information on Rachel Carson's childhood home, a National Register historic site. The Homestead offers educational programs based on Rachel's environmental ideals. Visitors can enjoy the surroundings that influenced Rachel's development and attitude toward the natural world.

www.pbs.org/moyers/journal/09212007/profile.html
This special presentation of *Bill Moyers Journal* looks at the life and legacy of Rachel Carson and her book *Silent Spring*, which launched the modern environmental movement. Of special interest is a compelling video featuring actress Kaiulani Lee. Ms. Lee performs a one-woman show about Rachel Carson.

www.time.com/time/time100/scientist/profile/carson03.html
Here is a full article about Rachel Carson as one of *Time* magazine's "Top 20 Most Influential Scientists and Thinkers of the 20th Century."

Index

About the Author

Patricia Lantier is the author of more than 30 books for children. A former educator and publishing executive, she currently enjoys working as a freelance writer and editor. She graduated with a bachelor's degree in English Education and a master's degree in English from the University of Louisiana–Lafayette, as well as a Ph.D. in English from Marquette University in Milwaukee. In addition to writing, she spends time creating jewelry, gardening, cooking Cajun food, and traveling. She lives in the beautiful Wisconsin countryside on several unspoiled acres of land with her husband Michael, an amazing array of wildlife, and a spectacular view of the night sky.